Split is an exquisite collection. These poems, haunting and life affirming, explore the body with ferocity and preciousness, at its most raw and precise. The melody of this body of work is eloquent and intimate calling us to witness the surrender and prayer-scream to an absent God, to messy family relations and to a literal hunger to consume the other with an intention not always offered the characters in this dish. The intensity left my cheeks flushed and grateful for the gift of this gothic femme poetics. What a powerful offering—a balm for the longing and living.

Maya Chinchilla, author of *The Cha Cha Files: A Chapina Poética*

What's a poem to god? What's a god to a mom? What's a parent to a non-believer? Benavides summons these questions with a sharpened rosary dipped in blood ink, half relic and half stake that meets the eyes with each poem that drives it into the heart of the matter: a riot girl is weaponized cavalry in herself. In a testament of poems wrestling the multitudes and facets of religion, daughterhood, sex, and _____ through candid language, Benavides's collection is an amalgamation of intense empathy and sorrow – not as a cause for alarm – but as intent to move and reclaim Self. These poems reveal to the lovers and past selves the balancing of one's inner light and darkness. The poems ask exhuming question-statements and answer back regarding our honest-to-goodness ungodliness.

Janice Lobo Sapigao, author of *Microchips for Millions*

Denise Benavides' writing is pure fire. The fire of rage, the fire of love, the fire of bodies refusing to shut up or sit still. From the flames the stories of mothers and daughters and lovers forge new voices and identities, with teeth and tears and tenderness. We need this book urgently. There is no other now.

Lidia Yuknavitch, award-winning author of
The Chronology of Water and *The Small Backs of Children*

SPLIT

SPLIT

Denise Benavides

Foreword by Elmaz Abinader

Kórima Press

The following poems first appeared in the publications noted below:

"El Color Rojo Significa Pasión" first appeared in *Foglifter Journal*, Volume #2, 2016.

"Throw The Women Back Into The Ocean" first appeared in *The Feminist Wire*, 2016.

"Love The Fag In You" first appeared in El Tecolote's 45th Anniversary Anthology: *Poetry in Flight / Poesía en Vuelo*, forthcoming–2016.

"Love Her, Leave Her" first appeared in *The Feminist Wire*, 2016.

"This House Is Empty Now" first appeared in *The Feminist Wire*, 2016.

"Saw A Woman In Half" first appeared in *FatCity Review*, 2013.

Cover Art
Title: "Skin is not a tough armor. It's soft, easily broken."
Artist: Jessica Sabogal
Medium: Spray Paint on Wood
Year: 2015
Artist website: jessicasabogal.com
Instagram: @jessicasabogal

Author photograph by Tomo Saito

Book Design: Lorenzo Herrera y Lozano

Published by Kórima Press
San Francisco, CA
www.korimapress.com

ISBN: 978-1-945521-01-0

for the women in my family.

CONTENTS

FOREWORD: BARBED WIRE AND HARP STRINGS

In the poetry collection, *Split*, Denise Benavides charts the path of blood flow—from mother to daughter, among sisters; in sexual actions and acts of violence. Every platelet reads like forensic evidence indicating proclivities, mental illness, dreams and connections: how do women survive love? Death? Loss? Abandonment?

It is time for the roll call: there are women present and those who are absent: ones with full minds, and some who are vacant and lost; there are those who feel love; most have lost it. Many are running, a few are sitting still. In *Split*, the encounters with, as the dedication states, the "women in my family," expose the very nature of being a woman—especially in the context of belonging—to a name, to a body, to a family and to a system. She claws the skin of truth to reveal a raw flesh below.

The four parts of *Split* present the poems in stages of healing: from prognosis, to diagnosis to treatment and then, rest and remedy. In Part One, we roam the rooms of houses, of hospitals, along the streets and find tenuous existences—the mother fades, the daughter runs, others fight or medicate in the face of brutality. These are not the common symptoms found in the confessional poems of tired lives—the suicidal rants and sorrowful weeping. Denise Benavides' women are slingers: armed with guns, rebellion, razors, drugs and tickets out of town. But then we wonder, how do they live without each other?

Go after them. The Poet follows the loss, the leaving and even the death. She brings the "little girl" to scrutinize the past and touch the wounds. The voice fears it will change her too much:

> i am not allowed to tell you about bell
> or my family
>
> or how many times
> ive had to change her name
> in these poems
>
> also, the little girl can no longer be _____
> in my poems.

she must be _____.

always be _____.

[from "This is Not the Death Poem You Asked For"]

These poems won't give in to death—the poems deal with tragedy but they don't wallow in the mire; the boots are put on, the steps taken, the branch held onto; strength is rebuilt. And as she says at the end of "This is How You Love Yourself":

> *i fear resistance.*
> *i fear no resistance.*

Denise Benavides has the words, the song, the witness and the feeling in the bones; the lies and revelations bundled in love knots and nooses, remedies and poisons. She, the poet, like the voice of the poems, is a solid force—her women don't weaken and neither do the poems in *Split*. Each line feels chiseled, etched into page and scratched along the insides of the mouth. You can hear the voice of the poet, as well as, her silences. Benavides' voice places us in the gears of the poems, whether they are couplets or puzzles, collaged or full of obedient lines, we hear the pronouncement of truth and history with decisive language and clean taut design.

The precision twining barbs and harp strings. In Part Three that meticulousness explodes and the shards cut with many edges. Love the Fag in You twists hate to vindication, to self-love to resignation:

> i am already forgetting
> what is even left
> between
> her
> and i

This voice is not self-pitying; this poet takes no shit. She lets the poem reflect on its own pain and throws some shade to the tribulations. In "The Weak Point," she minimizes the significance of the father, by trading off his identity, even with a passing stranger.

> *tell him you forgave him*
> *a long time ago*
>
> here, we will unpack the story—
> on this page
>
> we will use the fisherman
> as your father
> as your catalyst
> to a stronger narrative...

These poems are slender, shaping the surgical instrument that dissects these relationships and sutures the connection to religion, to work, to identity and to living. In the fourth section, the body is open, liberated from mitigating the pain of the past. The wisdom of survival and legacy shape a voice that takes on trauma and dilutes its power. From the titles alone, you can detect a strengthening of spirit and the voice lets us know that she knows, she finally knows:

> Fight
> *Abort the Father in You*
> *It Is Ok to Love Her Tonight*
> *This Is How You Show Your Love*

The movement of *Split* ties us into the necessity of losing your past, rebuilding it, and then re-creating the self-inside out. If there are secrets, we don't sense them because the language, even with its open blanks, is frank and refractive—*this is not an easy life, these are not easy people, but listen, I can handle it,* Benavides says.

In the years I have heard her stunning readings and studied her work, her shoulders have been against the wheel of the writing and the performing. While there is a star quality to the stage performances and a crispness to the poetry, the poet maintains a humility, a studiousness about how relationships, all relationships have softness, no matter how hard the exterior. This is true of Denise as well. These poems present both. They are stories as much as they are verse, compression of idea and inflammation of truth. Benavides helps us discover the slow process to understanding love, faith and leaving the dead alone.

Elmaz Abinader
Author of *This House, My Bones*
1 October 2016

SPLIT

PART I

YOUNG BLOOD
AND BURNING

im all matchbox
and dim lit heart
licking sand paper
waiting for the pick,
not knowing what
i was made for,
not knowing who
i was made for,
not knowing that
this/right now
was my turn
only knowing
i was next
to break away
from the mold
in this box
and breathe again,
or for the first time
but there are no
beautiful breakaways
just blacked out
car rides
and little girls
playing suck-back
with fingers pressed
and candied cigarettes
at their lips
waiting for their teeth
to set in

FOR TANYA

i was switched from prozac to fluoxetine
the me of then is gone forever

these are the questions i did not ask:
is genre friendly?
how muddy is the mississippi river?

i am dangerous in the dark,
nothing to see but a strung gallery of poetry inhibitions

in the meantime i store memories like neurotic folks do—
with empty bottles and faded magazines

then there's a film on tv about a good time girl,
she owns a cheap copy of the kama sutra

(i have an exaggerated sense of my own unimportance)

ticking and learning to live
with a thinning grip

DAILY RITUAL

no one
at the table
is smiling

my father
at the head

my mother
missing
her cue

i want to ask
why my hands itch

i want to ask
so much of them

i want to ask
how much
is safe

to swallow
at this age

i want to ask
how much of them

is safe

to swallow
at this age

EL COLOR ROJO SIGNIFICA PASIÓN

ive always believed that the universe
invented the color red for Latinas.
—Junot Díaz, This Is How You Lose Her

this is how you hedge down
the throat.

say, *hello*
to the precious pill
in your head.
the precious pills in your head—

there is a backlog of memory
in my head:
in my head:
in my head:

say human, again.

the wine spoils, momma.
you are a blanket of sad afternoons.

she is the first set of hips i raked
and left.

(i tear them whole. or not at all).

this is when you unlearn the starting over
this is when you get to start over

there is no more picking at your skin

you are the primal life force, child.

dig.

[red is the color of the catholic's crucifixion:
the same color they will associate with your
death.]

if a third hue were to exist: you would still be deliberate.
red.

HAPPY BIRTHDAY, MOM

my mother waited to tell me things,
kept them hung inside her like weights
until i was strong enough to carry
them in my own body.

she is fifty-seven years old today
and most days i still wonder
how many she has left

S L E E P

i lay the way i imagine jesus did
on the cross when he was finally lowered
days after they ran stakes through his palms—
arms outstretched just enough to reach
each side of the bed—and i imagine
breaking each one of my ankles
for this all to make sense. i don't know why
i do this, or why i remember
the dark circles my mother wore
the fatigue in her limbs, how much
of herself she bargained
and lifted up to him

MOTHER, ME
MOTHER, HER

you are a lifetime of work—
grapple with the layout

and feel, little girl:

i am the incarnate of my mother,
because of her i know
my femininity

because of her i know
the make up of my make up

because of her i know
a love worth
kneeling for

ON MEETING GOD

i ask him if he knows what drowning feels like,
the rush of salt—liquid begging to run through you.

i ask him if he's heard silence,
heat and metal—thunderclaps in his mouth.

i ask him the last time he felt the hum of an old spiritual hymn,
or the twitch of a real woman's thighs.

i ask him if he knows hunger,
or the reason for my mother's lies.

i ask him if he remembers the taste of breast milk,
or if he's ever held love in his palms.

i ask him if his father left him too,
or if he broke a promise with the levees.

i ask him if he gave up on us after hiroshima,
and if he was with me when i did my first line of coke.

i ask him if he ever grew tired of my grandmother,
or if his feet calloused after walking beside her.

i ask him if he's ever cat called a time bomb,
or if he's ever laid naked in time square.

but he only sits there—

half mooned here, the other on a bridge of lucid dreams
and i can't quite tell if he's listening.

GOD AND WHEN MY MOTHER PASSES

i imagine the red dress we have chosen
and asking the coroner
if we could be the ones to dress her

it is a still moment between sisters,
my mother on a metal table
and a clock swelling to just past three

karla will cup the back of her head
as we lift her—tanya will be down at her feet,
tugging the fabric toward us.

i am sure i will be the one zipping it
kissing the nape of her neck at the end—

i will blush her flushed cheeks,
and reach for the red lipstick
she's kept inside her purse
for special occasions

we will do all of this in silence
whimpering only when it hurts.

the men in my family will be
at the mouth of my grandmother's church
waiting to carry her in. my grandfather
will have come down from above
and be at the head of the casket;
finally walking his little girl down the aisle

the stained glass will drench the men
in blood orange and sky,
there will be beautiful lilies at every pew
the casket will be white
and those who loved her will wait
in line to pour their tender limbs over it—

her cold hands clutching my grandmother's crucifix,
a solemn decision karla will have made.

the women will hold what's left of the babes
in our family, cooing them in a blanket of sad afternoons.

i envy them—i envy their ability to sleep through this
and what little they know about the dead and mourning

and when the time comes, i will ask the coroner
if i could be the one to drive her. it will be summer
in ensenada with a blazing red heat and we will stop
at the pier that watched my mother grow up.

i will open the door and imagine her smiling
as the cool breeze of her favorite ocean
slips into her coffin.

we will drive around until the sun goes down

we will drive around just her and i
we will drive around just her and i

we will drive until the moon balloons
to just past perfect for a night like this

and when we arrive late to the cemetery,
no one will notice—and when the priest
has finished his sermon about
sorrow and the *undeserving*—
my lip will curl in anger
toward her and the most absent man
in my life will be there with me
as they lower her. he will hold my hand
and tell me it is happening; that she is done

hurting and for the first time
it will be how she wanted—he
will have asked her up to heaven,

and i will sit and watch
as the strongest and weakest
woman i have ever witnessed

leaves this physical world

LIKE THE FATHERS
WHO FORGOT THEM

we lived in blue grass and royal
we lived in sickle-celled minds
and glass gallows—two young girls
and a banjo

we'd sing a cappella
if they let us

we'd bring earthquake in our hips—
rockabilly to the streets

hoping the loose boys of the block
would throw in a little more
than _____ .

two young girls
too young girls

JOLLEEN

kurt and cocaine white
lilies hang from her window
after the spin has stopped
after all the records
lay numb alongside us

we lay there, humming—
caressing the floor

too many lines deep
to remember the lyrics
of his sad songs

we are only sixteen
but we have been sad
for so long

i ask her if she believes
in nights not meant for sleeping
and how many creases
she'll fold into her skin
before she looks
in the mirror
and sees

a hollowed resemblance
between her and the carcass
lying naked and unadorned
in the middle of the street

she isn't more than
a bag of bones
frozen and headless

crawling closer to the dust
that huddles under a post
for warmth

THE WOMEN IN MY FAMILY

are hard and strong, made up of iron
and too much stone around their laugh lines

they are the backbone, weight bearers
and frontline soldiers of my family—

gun slung and stretched over their wombs,
without them there is no man

or room for scraps—just pig
outstretched in his own muck and shit

fat and heavy—without them
man is foul

without them man is dick hung low
man is dick unused

PUPPET

she is wearing the smile
ive grown to know
over the years

it is the one that sits
at the table

sips chilled zinfandel
out of a cardboard box

and stretches
catholic at the cue,

at the over indulged
eyes of my father

at the tug and sway
of the puppeteer

HOW TO GET AWAY FROM THE FATHER

she said, i thought he'd killed us,
but look: we are alive

       —Lidia Yuknavitch

i know what it is like
to go mad here—

to piece back memory
like a fracture

you: only a _____
a familial game we played

do you remember how i bled
in that hallway?

the way i pulled
your stomach
out of my body

and used language
as a tool that day—

i bargained for words
that day

together we reached
the diction of our name—

                        twenty years later
                           i no longer
                   bleed in that hallway

twenty years later
i learned to follow
the blood trail back
into the body

twenty years later,
sweet mother

i could have sworn
i was actually alone that day

twenty years later,
sweet mother

you, in your silence
in the other room

me, in the way
i no longer absorb it

like a blueprint
like a pact
deciding to live in me

a struggling life, and death
this is how we both learned to forget

RULE #8

in an abandoning circumstance,
detach first.

learn to detach, first

YOUNG BOY

i watch him grapple with the needle
and wait for the guttural sound of his throat to wake

i want him sad and lonely, i think—

i want him left the way old dog dessa
and pop's gun shook,

i hope this is making sense to you

i want him left like all the lost boys
have gone home, but him

i want him sad and lonely, i think—

this poem is for the boys who play violin
pale with addiction, pretending
to be _____ .

i hope this is making sense to you

this poem is for the boys
only i and the carnival
dare to adopt

WHEN YOU FORCE THE FORM

reset
before you _____

tell them
how you found the trigger

how you learned
to put your lips there

how you're done kneeling
in their church

how in your library

it is always
8:44pm

PART II

L O L I T A

stop picking apart
the small woman inside you

toss her a hook, line in a poem

name her a good name—*lolita*
the name of the little woman
that mocks and writhes inside you

mommy's little flower
is just a child
just a church hymn

you keep her
under your grandmother's tongue

fingering the rosary stuck inside you

you are always just stuck inside *you*

she tells you, you are the only
freckled granddaughter

how you are nothing more than
a consequence of bait

your mother, a fire

your father, a never stand still soil

this is the blood that built you, little girl
do not forget the blood that built you, little girl—

i am a humble, but persistent terrorist
of this body

always in search of _____.

when i feel it close, i slant harder

tell her, they make women
different these days

no back pocket
to keep my mother in

no back pocket
to keep my father in

i tell her
i am ok being the one
that stays up at night

i am ok being the one
that births lolita back at night

back into each one of our poems,

tell her that in the morning
you will love her like sugarcane

and in the evening
you will kill her like sugar came

i admit, i am still learning
to love her—lolita dead

me, born again

WHERE CROWS GO TO DIE

i woke up to a crow
pecking the window of my bedroom

she stood bow legged—astounded
by the reflection of her condition

her left eye dangling
fresh flesh hanging from her neck

and i could have sworn
this had happened before

she had come here before

the crook of her feathers, the smell
of a good fight on her beak—

i want to clean her up, i think

i want to hold her
juvenile in my hands, the way
i imagine mothers do

i want to maroon her neck in mine
the way i imagine lovers do

but she is too proud—too heated
from the fight, dipping her head
threatening

to jump the ledge

LITTLE GIRL

tell me all the ways
the pilgrim loves his son

i want you to build
a home there

i want you to pick up
the trajectory—your mood change

i want you to buy into the story

discomfort comes
in the form of a howl:
how many times
have you howled, little girl?

shawn lives seven years back,
but claudia still loves him

because claudia knows how to keep the emotional vein from popping
learn to keep the attention level at an eight, little girl

this isn't how mother did it

mark here, and here, little girl.

ask,

"when is it appropriate
to cut into the head?"

HER LOVE STAYS

she is my warm
revolving storm

the eye of her
traps itself
sharing my cage

the world: *envelope*
on its knees
bows to her—

i bow to her

my sweet law,
i pocket her rage

she is the small good
i have found in my mother

act of her balancing act
her love knows how to stay

do you hear me?

she knows how to stay.

SWALLOW

clear off the table, little girl

put your grandmother there
in that chair, little girl

cup her hand in yours—
guide her, little girl

press fork to tongue
and let her mouth
food from plate, little girl

no, like *this*
little girl

she deserves to swallow
small, and whole

THROW THE WOMEN
BACK INTO THE OCEAN

i want to rename her
something blue
like the night
she was forced into

i want to rename her
something life-form
like *rib*, or *muscle*—

i want to rename her
something like *sleeping*,
or *breathing*

wear her like
a blood work of veins

anything but
a stomach
hollow enough
to carry a family
of secrets

i want to tell her
this place
is where you trace
your hand back

where you go blind
imagining scissors

i want to tell her
mother, this is no place
to store a body

i want to tell her
mother, you and i
are something
water born

i want to tell her
mother, you and i
are something
worthy of preservation

do you hear me?

THIS IS NOT THE DEATH POEM YOU ASKED FOR

i am not allowed to say _____ in my poems anymore.

i am not allowed to use *blood,* or *fuck,* or *god*
in my poems anymore.

i am not allowed to tell you about _____,
or how many times ive knelt down to pray for his death.

i was told _____ was taking up too much space in my head
that the poems of him were getting weaker, more *predictable*—

not allowed to tell you the questions i would ask
when _____ came back

i am not allowed to mention _____ abuse, or depression

not allowed to imagine my _____'s funeral
or consider the lilies i would crown each pew with

she has to be healthy, smiling
more pretending for the poems—

i am not allowed to tell you about bell
or my family

or how many times
ive had to change her name
in these poems

also, the little girl can no longer be _____
in my poems.

she must be _____.

always be _____.

THIS IS HOW YOU LEARN TO MOTHER YOURSELF

the thing is,
this is what i'm not suppose to tell you:

former addicts never
write to stay clean, and
former addicts never really
enjoy the stuck
little child of misery

former addicts birth
the little child back
into a mixture
of shame and history

dare not name
the child
a good name

dare not admire
the way both can coexist
in a body made of blame

[this is where you can change the perspective,
slant the truth a little louder.]

i fear resistance.
i fear no resistance.

FEEDBACK

my mother is losing her mind. [great opening line.]
my mother is losing her mind. [   ]
my mother is losing her mind. [develop this].
my mother is losing her mind. [what's another way of saying this?]
my mother is losing her mind. [too telling.]
my mother is losing her mind. [yes, but how can you complicate this?]
my mother is losing her mind. [this doesn't sound like your other work?]
my mother is losing her mind. [too quiet.]
my mother is losing her mind. [is this metaphorical?]
my mother is losing her mind. [have you considered your readership?]
my mother is losing her mind. [yes, but what message are you trying to relay?]
my mother is losing her mind. [didn't you already write this poem?]

my mother is losing her mind. [is this the turn?]
my mother is losing her mind. [not too sure this is a strong enough ending.]

INTIMACY COMES IN RELIGIOUS FORMS

el beso
en la mejilla,
el significado de la cruz

every morning
etched
from third eye
chest to shoulder

every morning
hushed lips
over my mother's
hand bones

this is what love
looks like

O X Y T O C I N

this is exactly how you leave
the nape of your neck exposed

pull back—

look ahead
i know, i know

this is just another one of my poems—
an elegant arranging of contradictions

but does it make you
uncomfortable yet?

is it because
i lack your restraint?

you, my holistic drug

bank:

a molecular mass of 1007.9 g/mol
a neuromodulator in the brain
a mechanism that enacts in moments of extreme bonding

are you bonding properly, little girl?

promote ethnocentric behavior, remember
to incorporate trust
to bond

these are all the things i wish i would have said

WHO WILL LOVE THE FATHER IN YOU?

i am
still trying
to decide
where
the line
breaks.

still trying
to decide
how to
brake

where
the line
breaks

like
father,
like
break.

WHAT SCARES YOU MOST?

1. the curtains in my bedroom
2. age eight
3. my sisters and their pieces
4. looking less and less like my mother
5. looking more and more like my mother
6. swallowing secrets
7. what would've happened if i hadn't slept
8.
9. my father in the kitchen, palming my sister's hair—dirty dishes
10. losing my _____
11. how many times i've imagined my _____
12. maybe it wasn't even whiskey he drank _____
13. how many poems are left
14. my grandmother and her _____
15. driving over tracks
16. the kettle
17. *inhale*
18.
19. how many times i've said *in my mouth, please*
20. dropping the wine
21. the ocean, losing—
22.

PART III

LOVE THE FAG IN YOU

there is a plate
of food
in front of me,
a chair
i sit in
hurled over
and a mother
across a table
explaining
the hate she has
for the fag in me

i tell her, smug
you are the fag in me

as she wades in a dull pain
bloated,

stagnant/thighed

her body is embodied in mine—
her body is embodied in mine.

i want to pickle her
in rosewater—

in the love
that does not tender
its shoulder to me

in the love
that leaves me
short sided

between
what is left
and
the barely
audible
distance between
her and i

i am already forgetting
what is even left
between
her
and i

FAITH, THE PERVASIVE PATH

learn to negotiate between force
and jawbone—

learn to negotiate your way out
with language, and not with language.

a conscious decision between
looking up
and scripture—

learn to confuse the poem
with scripture

let the god reside on the page,
and build your faith there

this is where
you dismantle
the father:

a cut,
reduction of a man.

the father
who can't help
but love

the break

you, who can't help
but love

the break

walk passed the pervasive path,

it is never pretty,
but there is _____ there

a consumption of communion

like sip back,
like wine, like
baby, like little girl

church is never the great equalizer.

THIS IS HOW YOU SACRIFICE THE BODY

this is how you let him bind elbow to back, little girl

let the buckskin hold you back, little girl
let the white-hot spare you, little girl

let the white hot light blister
let the white hot robe of your father
hover, little girl

this is how you become sacrificial,
little girl

HOW THE MUSIC STOPPED

she was ordinary

like one of those
5 o'clock
time punchers,
get home at 8
after some brews
and a couple of those
jukebox *baby, you hurt me*
real bad tunes

until she wasn't.

until she stood there,
in your kitchen
with the dirty linoleum
and broken glass

holding a pair of pumps
and one of those
thin rubber hoses
that make your veins pop—

until she wasn't.

WITH MY PERMISSION I

after "Letter to My Heart from My Brain"
by Rachel McKibbens

it is ok to pulse one by one
today

it is ok to hold your breath
underwater
and let it all out

to call this *rock bottom*

and it is ok to ask
the betty page bartender
for the house special
and fuck her

ok to change your name
in the morning

to call this *catholic guilt*—

and it is ok to forget your mother
leave her for dead, the way
the fisherman did

and it is ok to howl at the dog
inside the home you'll never have

and it is ok to wait for the fisherman
to come back with eyes closed

LA LEONA

she is your bad october
addiction

the borrowed bed
you spend
fucking
every girl in

she is all thirteen
of your severed heads

a mother mountain of lions—

you learn to build into her
at a small age

she the pot-bellied pig
that feeds and kills your village

the lion/mother
you are so desperate
to protect

THE WEAK POINT

the man in the cinema smiles at me,
an ordinary assault in effect.

but here, we will speak of universal truths:

like where you learned to hold
the memory down

like the way father goes
from child to child

tell him you forgave him
a long time ago

here, we will unpack the story—
on this page

we will use the fisherman
as your father
as your catalyst
to a stronger narrative

i can't really control the narrative.
i'm not the one controlling the narrative.

we will use _____ to cut into the body
the way religion cuts into the body—

the way religion finds a weak point in the body

[it all sounds so biblical. even
when it's not.]

the mind is a powerful tool.
even when it's not.

CUT OUT THE FATHER IN YOU

let her dig her toes in

let the blood drip—move it

all this back and forth
wont lessen the story

though i imagine
this is how
you overwhelm your audience—

mark the trees

limp, run, jump
until you find her

learn how to find her

and when you are done learning
hang the body, here

cut out the father-bone

keep in mind the writing
gets messy here

the drought
is always the most
dramatic point

WHY JESUS NEVER SAVED ME

tell me about the bishop, mother.
tell me how he pulled your organs
over
one by one

before he did it

tell me about the pew you sat in—
the mahogany in that wood

how he hovered his milk white drone
over your belly—

before he did it

tell me how he whispered
from a high point—

jesus will save you

into your little girl ear
before he did it

tell me your body
is old like language
in proximity to mine

promise me that jesus didn't ask him
to savor little girls like wine

PART IV

I HAVE LEFT ROOM FOR YOU

from the old crows
you have carried
and thrown
over your shoulder

to the bone fingers
that entered like dead souls
over the small of my back

they have meant so little to you;

they have been raked
for flesh and gnawed on
by the jowls
of hungrier _____ ,

i know.

they beat
and cower
to the rough sea
inside your chest;

your backbone betrays you

and in this room
you have left them

and for one moment
i hold them, *beloved*

hoping to see
them rise

WAIT

i knew a girl
once. she said
she takes _____
to stop the lying
she said
the five-dollar an hour
psych student
she sees once a week
told her to stop

to let the demon in

to wait for the wrap
of his knuckles
at the door—

to expect him
calm and dull

and maybe that's not
what i was told

but these poems
and the lying
never stop
and the girl,
the little girl
with the horrible
horrible _____

never stopped

LIKE THE VIOLENT DO

love me like the violent do

i want to feel it
in your tongue thrash

the way you carry it
in your rasp

i want to hear it
in your father's belt—

the way it buckled
and unbuckled

i want it
like all the lonely boys
have gone home—

like each one
learning
to love me
like the violent do

FIGHT

i imagine her death every day—

a bridge
railroad tracks
maybe a murder
or drowning
a kitchen knife
poison
an overdose

diving the way birds do
dying like little girls do

in my poems

there is always
an unstoppable force
coming after them,

i come after them
so others wont

learning to want
the bite

learning to like
the fight

ABORT THE FATHER IN YOU

my stage is in this corner
of light—the dark
edge of light

watch me
as i spare you

this is all intentional—

the rock back and forth—let,
leave and love the comeback

*you, who never learned
the comeback*

i am your quiet
confident, ghost baby

tell me—did you know
what the consequences were
for a fashioning death?

tell me—would you
have asked the doctor
if it would be surgical,
or medical at this point?

would the fetus know?

IT IS OK TO LOVE HER TONIGHT

turn this key into this light.
turn this key into this light.
turn this key into this light.
turn this key into this light.
turn this key into this light.
turn this key into this light.
turn this key into this light.
turn this key into this light.
turn this key into this light.
turn this key into this light.
turn this key into this light.
turn this key into this light.
turn this key into this light.
turn this key into this light.
turn this key into this light.

THIS IS HOW YOU SHOW YOUR LOVE

i'd eat her left rib first,
if she let me

i'd spread the meat
of her thighbone
teeth to muscle
every night,
if she let me—

reach through her clavicle
down to her heart
and feel it struggle,
if she let me

pop a vein, sip wine
from her blood
every night,
if she let me

rip the skin
between lip
and numb,
if she let me

i swear, i'd suck
her rosed cheeks
pale like addiction,
if she let me

and i'd promise to love
and love, and love
the savor
in her marrow
most,

if she let me.

THIS HOUSE IS EMPTY NOW

i am sure this is the poem
i will write after you have left

our bed is a small
and empty birdcage
in the mouth of a snake

the blood we shared and left
in the cupboard
thickens

and the drains keep reaching
for handfuls of your hair

the animals we raised
skinned and hung themselves today

and the hinges on the door
have forgotten your name

but each nail howls
at the thought of it—

the chimney, riddled with worry
has broken all of its front teeth

the ghost in the hallway
speaks ill of our blame game

desperate for affection
the windows stay open

i stay open

i want to wail with the old grief
you left under the sink

i want to wail, *i want you back*
with me

your love—the only thing
i refuse to keep

WHO IS RESPONSIBLE FOR THE SUFFERING OF YOUR MOTHER?

she is.

SEARCHING FOR GOD

i hold her rosary in my palm
and don't recognize
the man hanging from it

his eyes have faded
and his crown is without thorns
worn down by the sweat
of my grandmother's thumb

every night, she'd kneel
like an old lover
praying for the better of us
praying that one day
i'd recognize his face

MOTEL ROOM

i gutted the *morning* after that night

held her tight by the crown
and emptied her
of all that swallowed moon shine
from the night before

and i wish i would have explained it
she didn't understand—

all i wanted
was one more hour
full of this darkness,
of this dancing and dipping
naked across the bedroom floor
cracked out of my mind
in this roach egg infested
motel room
that one weekend
where i wasn't
more than a child waltzing
on my toes

and i wonder if she still remembers me
waltzing on my toes?

and i know these poems are getting old

but there was so much midnight
in my eyes
and all i want to do
is sleep a thousand times

TELL ME

tell me about the one that triggers most
your father

tell me about the tips of his fingers

the point in which they come to
when he speaks to you

the resemblance in their walk
the air they let *out*

tell me, *hope*

tell me that his jawline
is not the one you crawl out of
every morning
in the mirror

and that the sound
that pours out of you
was not his, first

tell me, *hope*

tell me that you speak
three languages
and that love resides
in your home

tell me that he never
held a fist to your mother

that his god has come back—
that he wrapped his knuckles
around your door, first

tell me how his apology
took form

tell me, *hope*

[Untitled]

let this poem not be about your mother.
let this poem not be about your mother.
let this poem not be about your mother.

i wonder how often he thought of me.
or the moment i realized i wasn't mine.

the moment i realized i took his bones without asking
hooked his tongue around my neck and left him backless
without a hand to hold.

how many years it took her to grow old,

i wonder about the intrepid in our tongue

how much pussy we've eaten—thick and clumsy with rage

i wonder about the moment i realized i could age.

the moment i preferred the feast
my own body could make.

i don't think this is how you write a poem
i don't think you're suppose to leave so much out

this is when you develop the story.

this is when you tell them about the kettle.
how you don't care about your regrets—
how lately you've kept a gun tucked under your bed

this is when you tell them about the time
you and bell fucked to pounding and breath

this is when you tell them about that one night
you felt god inside you.

this is when you tell them
about how many more of us are left

WITH MY PERMISSION II

after "Letter to My Brain from My Heart"
by Rachel McKibbens

it is ok to believe in the monk and not the messiah.

it is ok to love the joker and not the game.

it is ok to love your father at night
when no one is awake.

it is ok to love the junkie and the hepburn in your sister
when you realize the junkie loves all three of us sisters.

it is ok to fear the mother in you. ok to waste away
in the hallway of the first apartment you ran away to

it is ok to fear his makeup in your makeup
until it feels ritual—until it is swollen
and warm/with wine.

and it is ok to love, and love,
and love even after the joker has left you
blind.

LOVE HER, LEAVE HER

shame killed my mother
first.

it was an allegory of deaths—

one
after the other

the bodies
becoming
a rebirthing
from the wastes

yet, i must grieve
each woman
honestly

in a desperate attempt
to say:

come back,
try your natural self
first.

WHEN LOVE ARRIVES,
THE DOOR WILL BE CLOSED

out into the ether,
somewhere

there is someone

there is her—

a metaphor
for the open
and the close—

a metaphor
that will coax the lions
back into the water

there will be so much water
in her.

About Denise Benavides

Denise Benavides is an Oakland-based queer xicana performance artist, poet, and radical educator sharing her work with urgency. Bred from a single immigrant mother, she uses the stage/page to confront themes of xenophobia, relocation, mental illness, sexuality, religion, and love. Always, love.

Denise writes to document, to archive, and to hold space for what has been lost—most of all, she writes for the women in her family.

Denise holds a Bachelor of Arts in English and a Master of Fine Arts in Creative Writing from Mills College. Her work can also be found in Third Woman Press' zine *Gonna Be Alright (Vol. 2)*, *Fat City Review*, *Ground Protest Poetry*, *El Tecolote*, *The Feminist Wire*, and *Foglifter Journal*. For more information on Denise Benavides, please visit: www.denisebenavides.com.

OTHER KÓRIMA PRESS TITLES

Amorcito Maricón
    by Lorenzo Herrera y Lozano

The Beast of Times
    by Adelina Anthony

Brazos, Carry Me
    by Pablo Miguel Martínez

The Cha Cha Files: A Chapina Poética
    by Maya Chinchilla

Ditch Water: Poems
    by Joseph Delgado

Empanada: A Lesbiana Story en Probaditas
    by Anel I. Flores

Everybody's Bread
    by Claudia Rodriguez

Las Hociconas: Three Locas with Big Mouths and Even Bigger Brains
    by Adelina Anthony

Jotos del Barrio
    by Jesús Alonzo

The Possibilities of Mud
    by Joe Jiménez

Salvation on Mission Street
    by Cathy Arellano

Tragic Bitches: An Experiment in Queer Xicana & Xicano Performance Poetry
    by Adelina Anthony, Dino Foxx, and Lorenzo Herrera y Lozano

When the Glitter Fades
    by Dino Foxx

Made in the USA
Lexington, KY
15 February 2017